This

COLORING BOOK

BELONGS TO

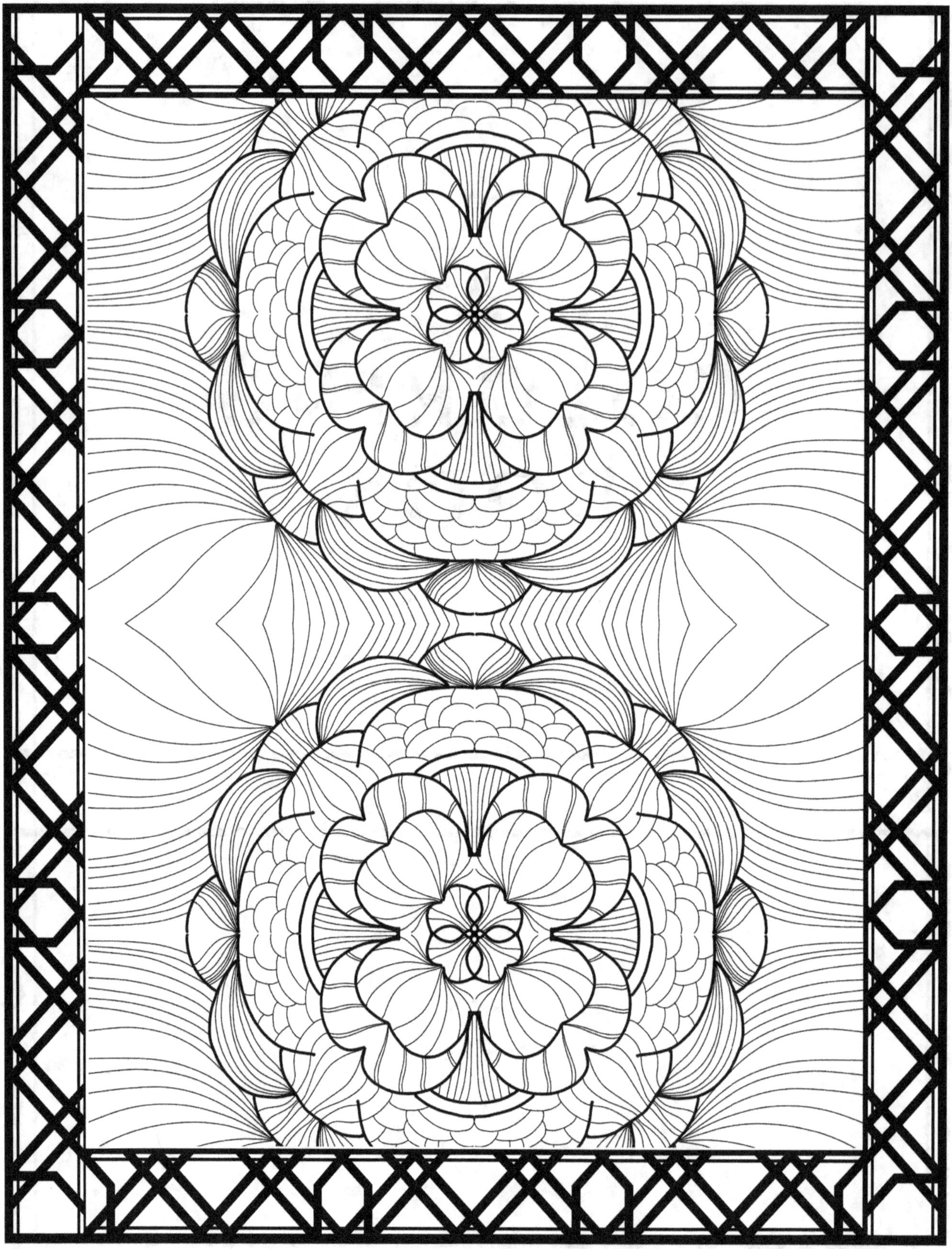

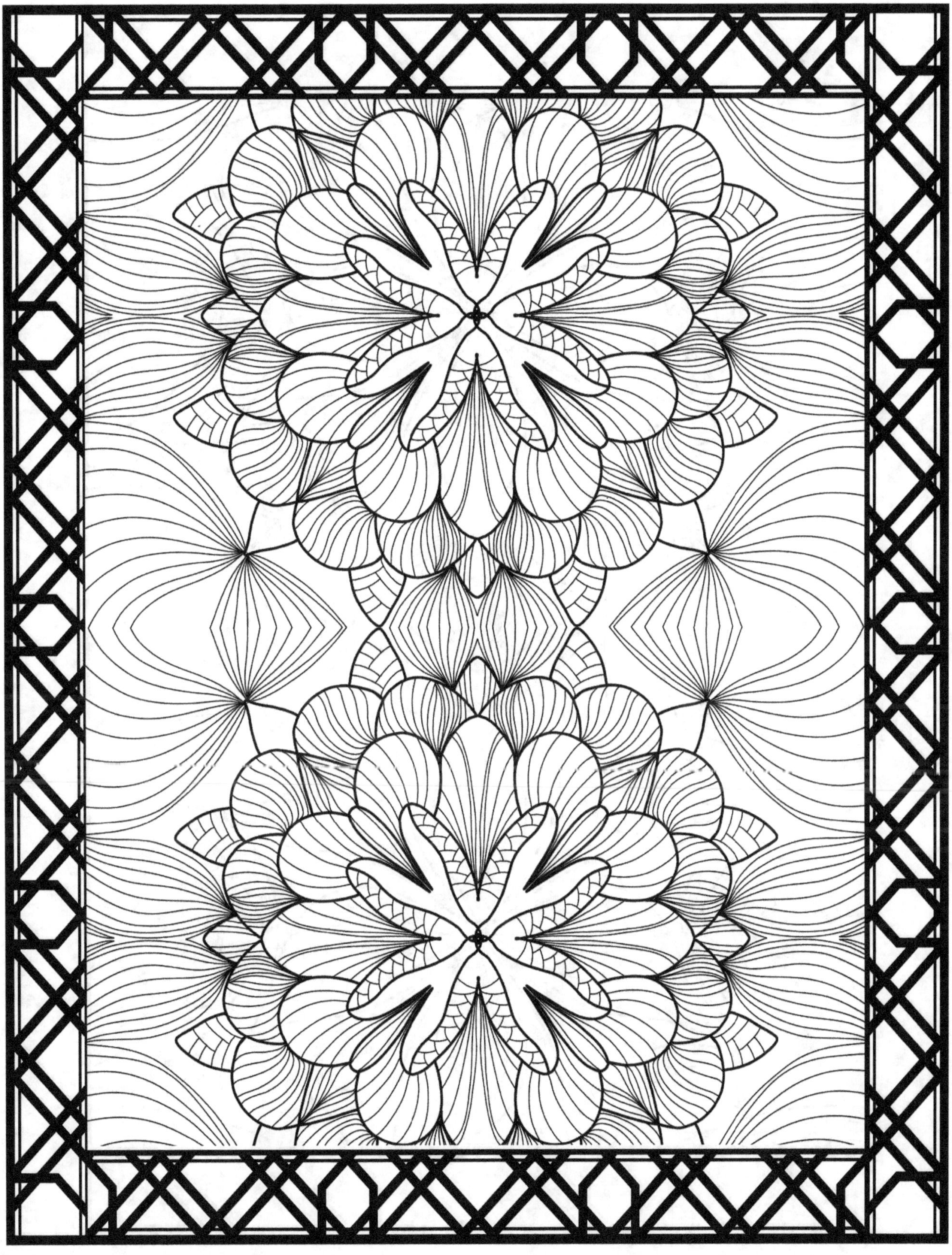

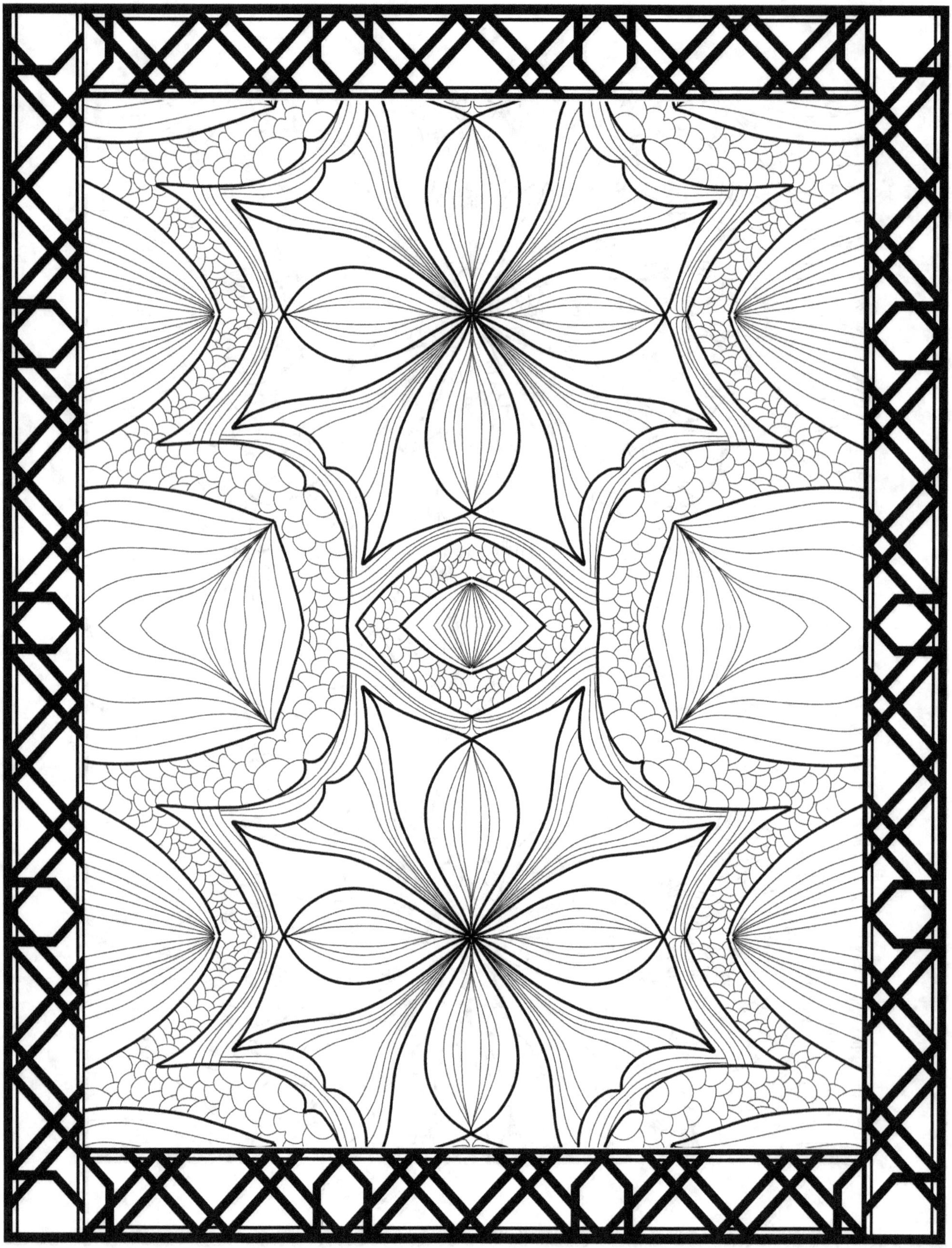

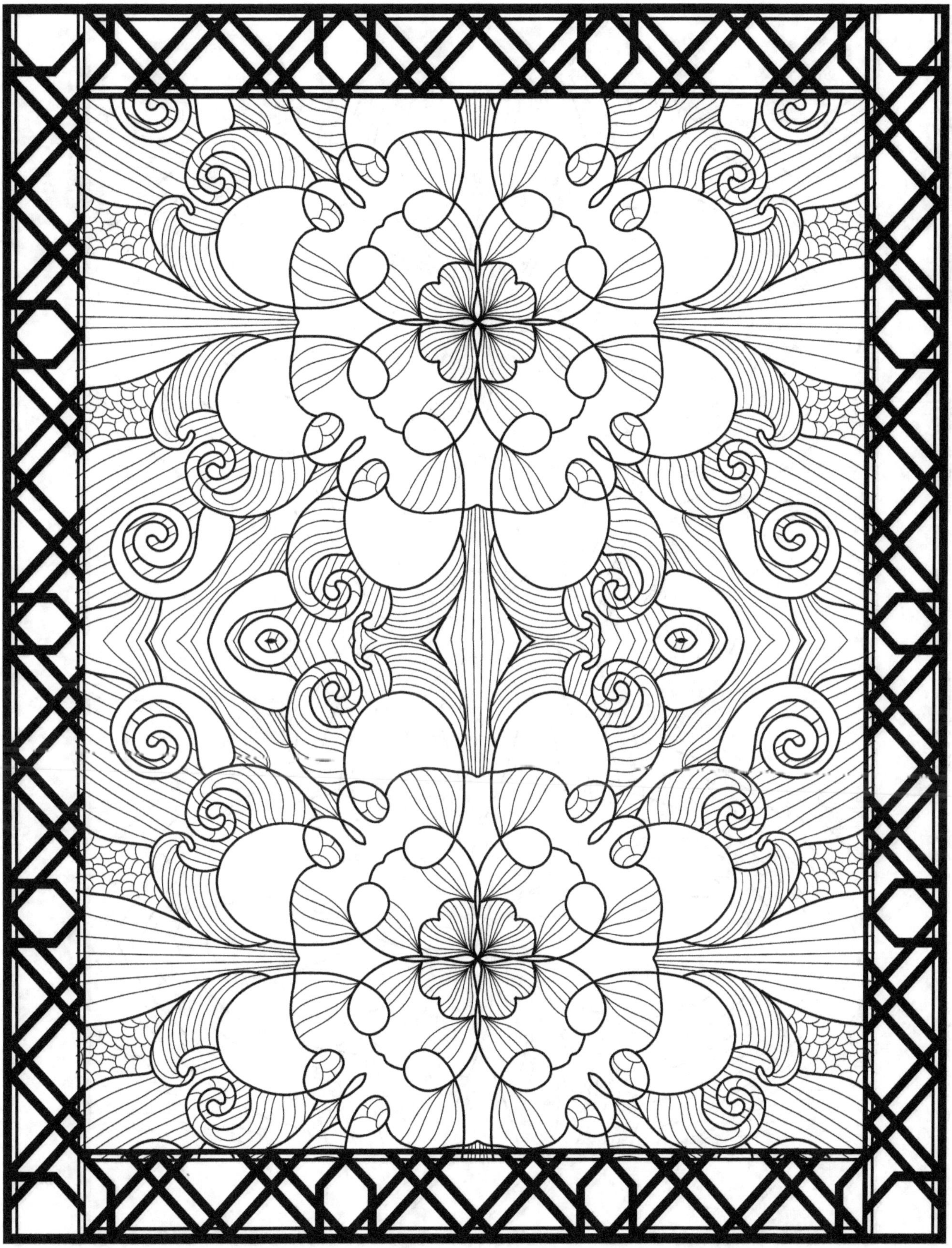

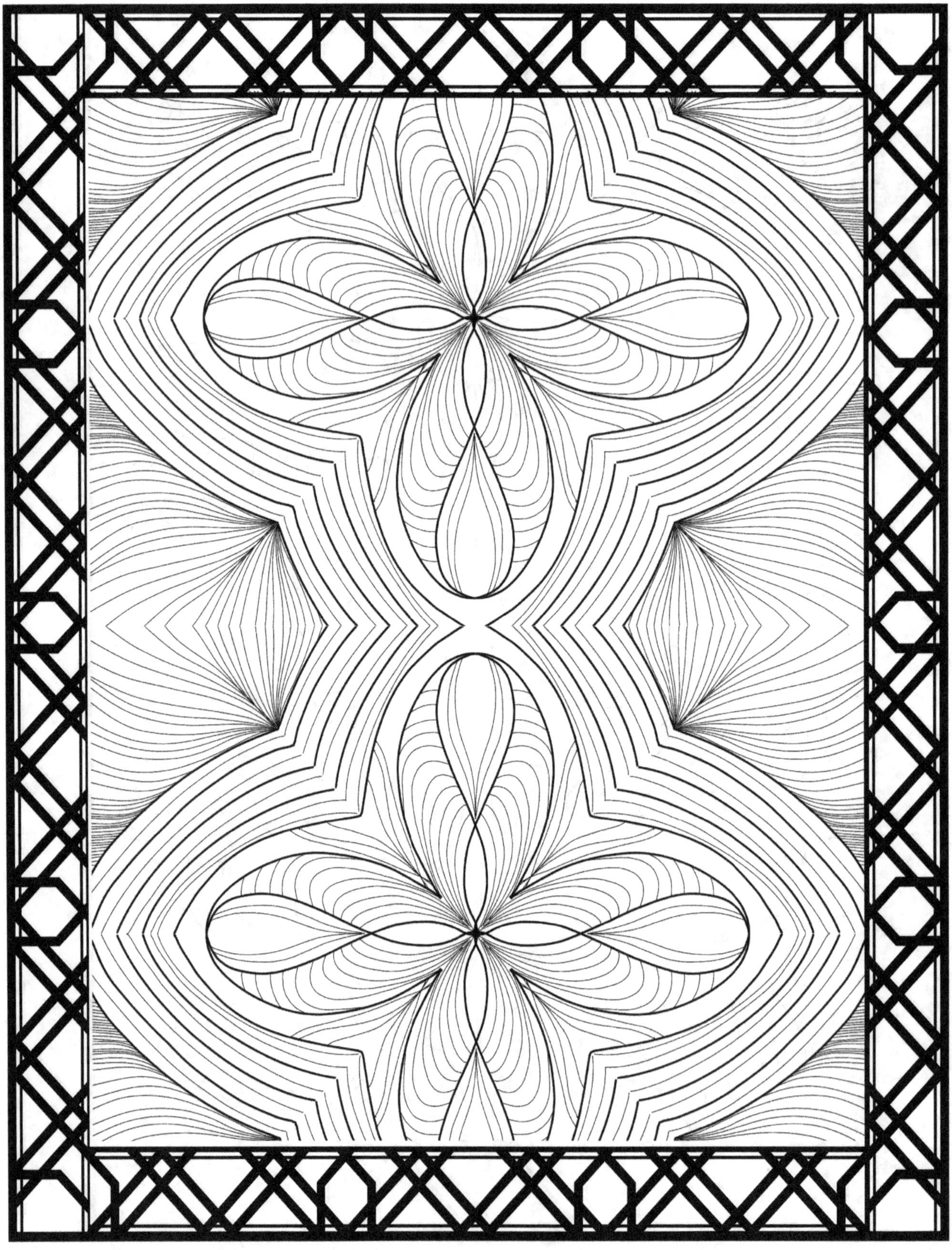

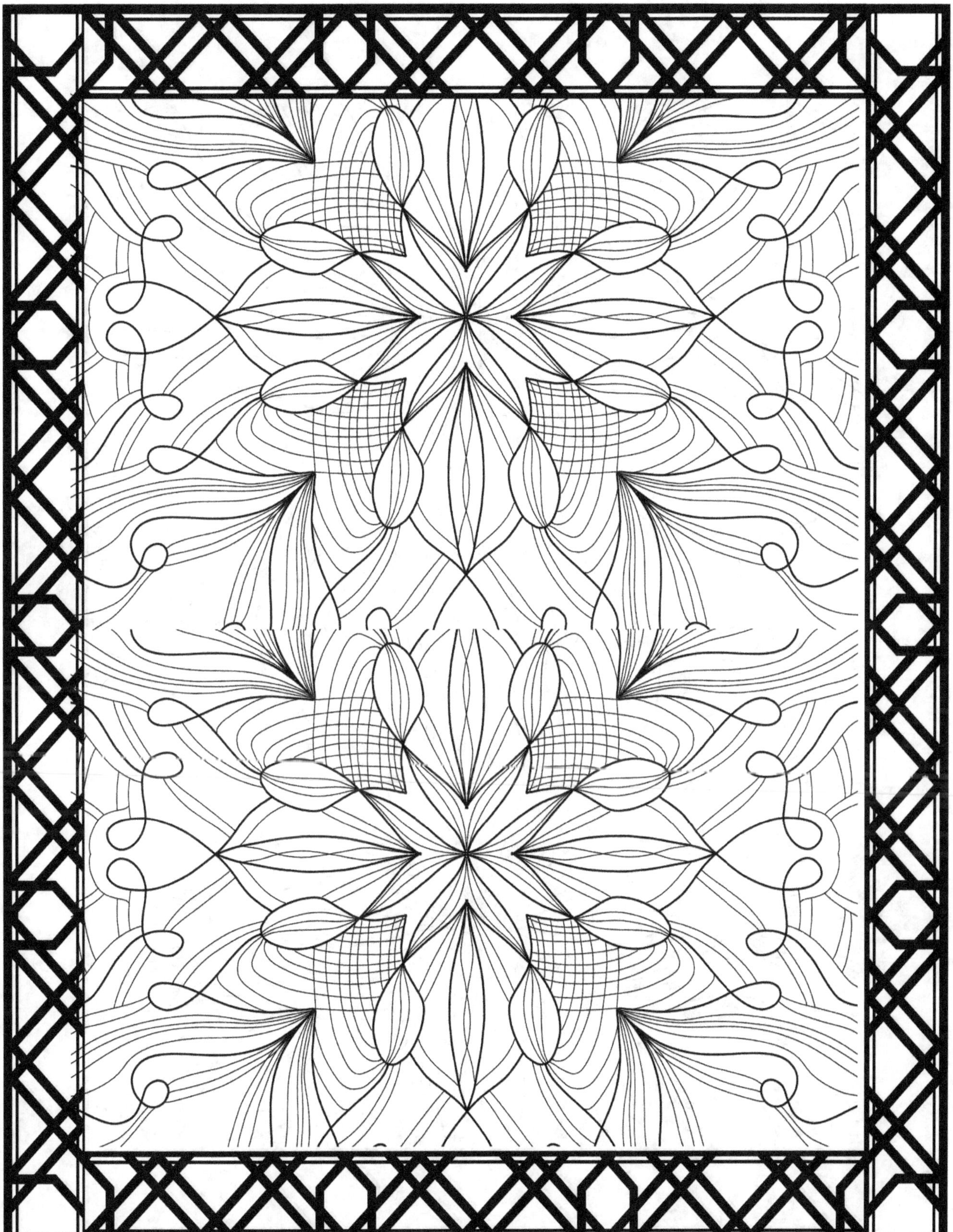

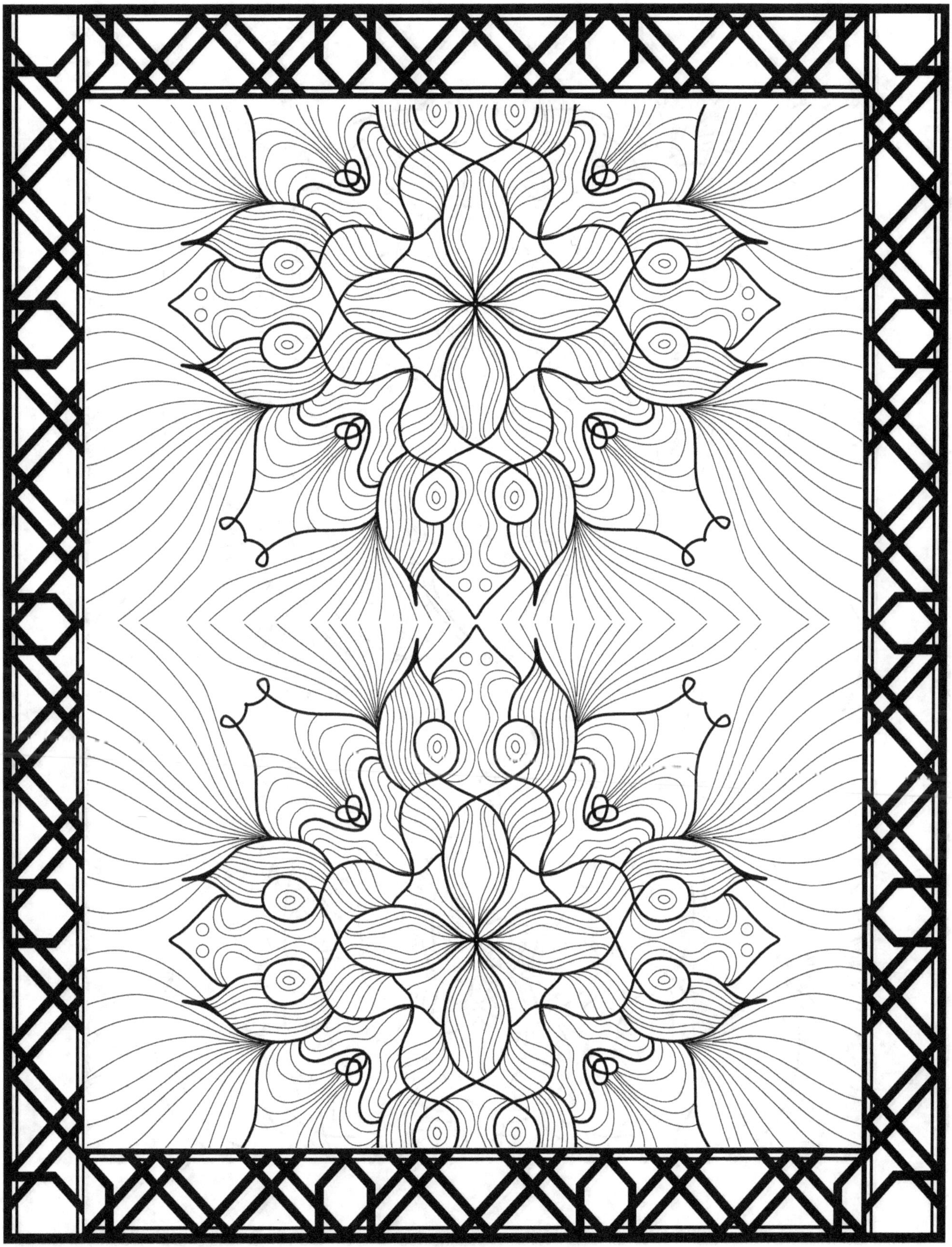

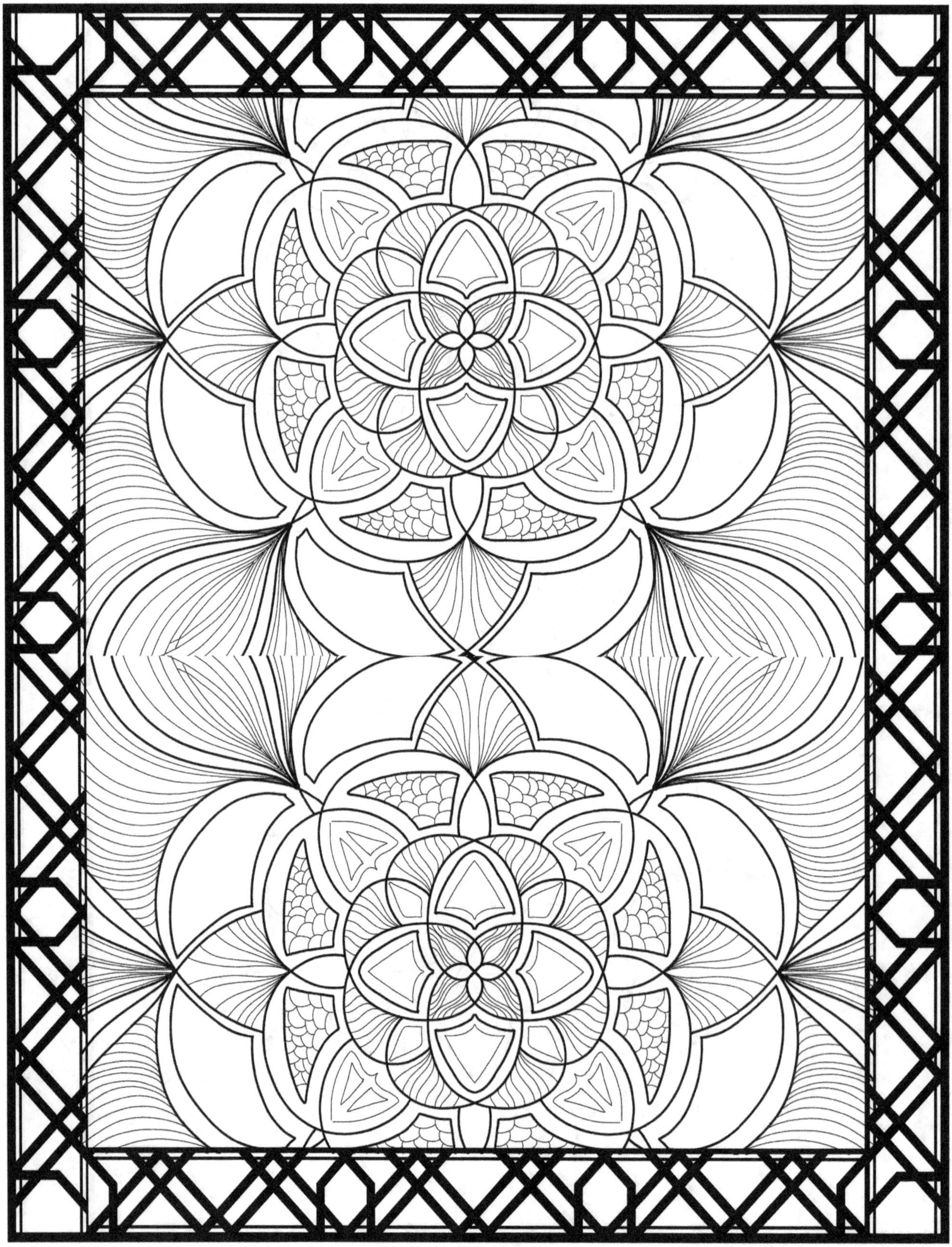

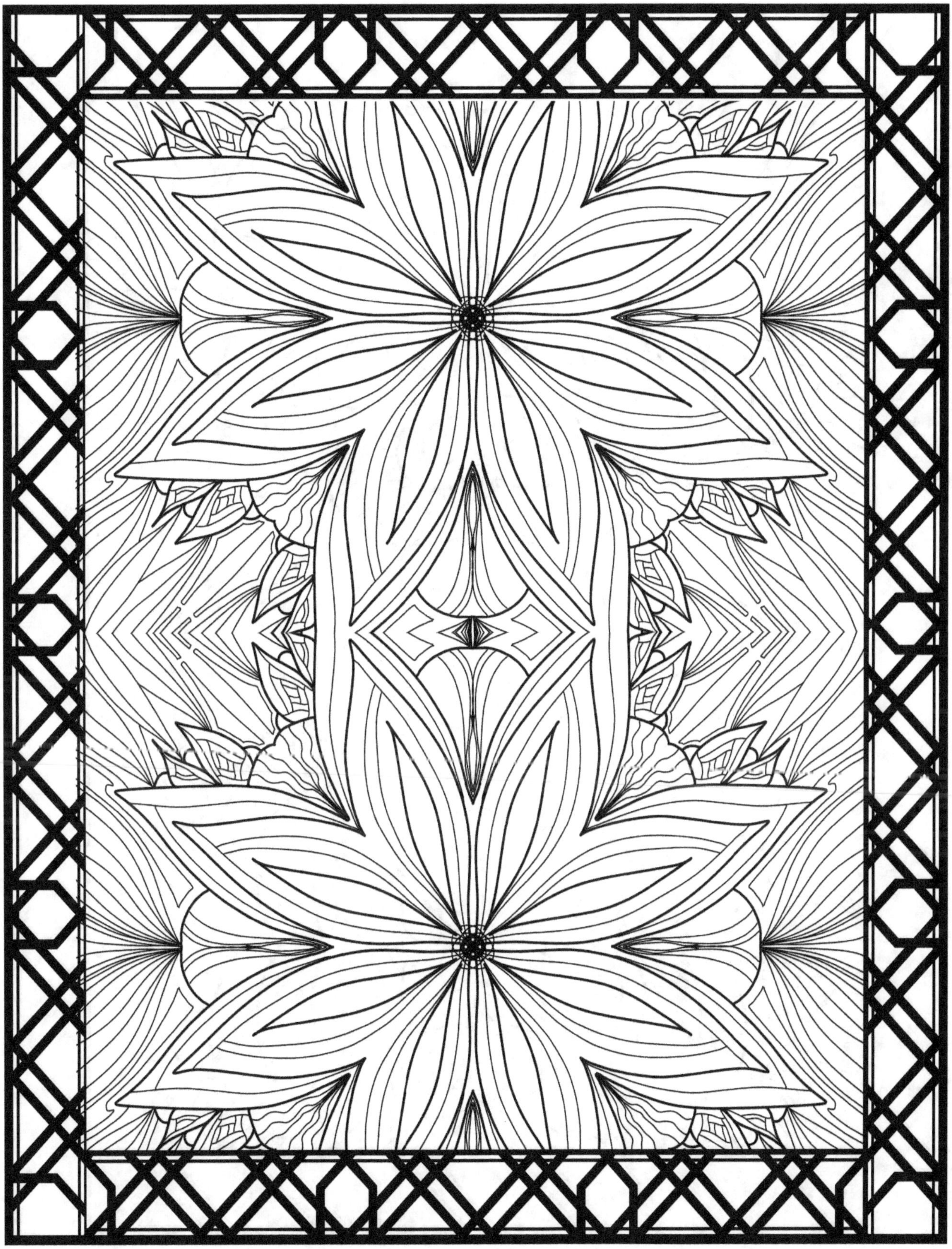

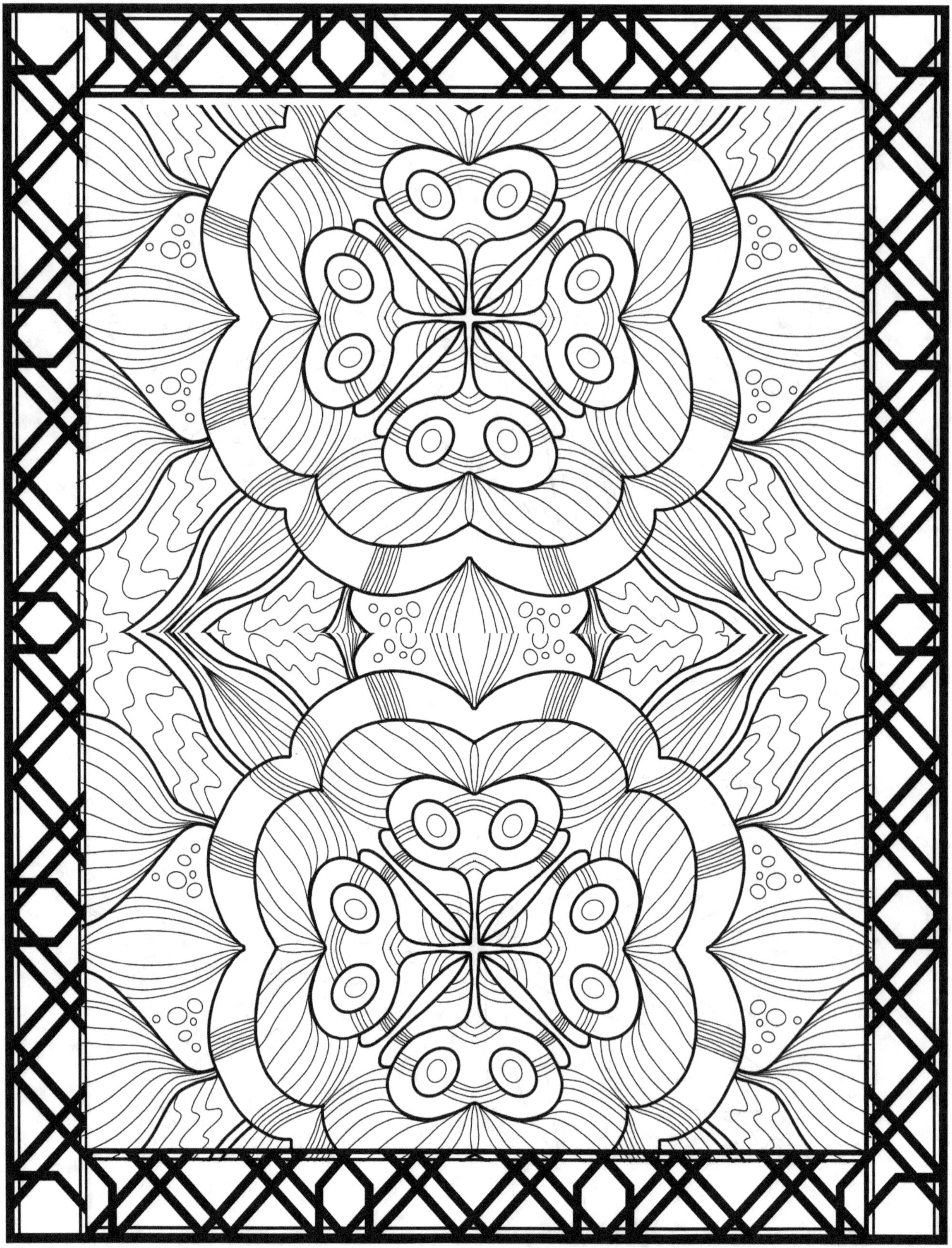

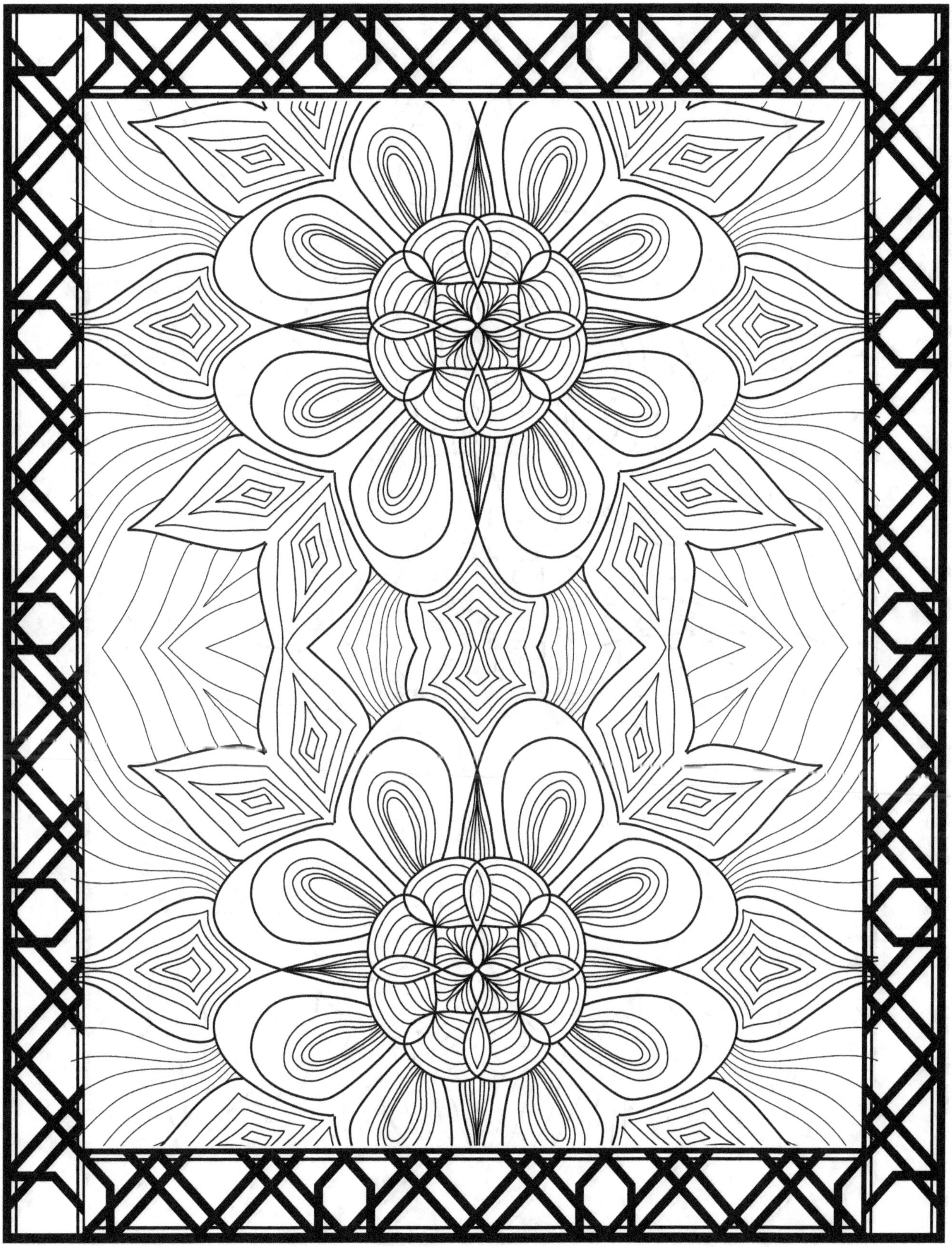

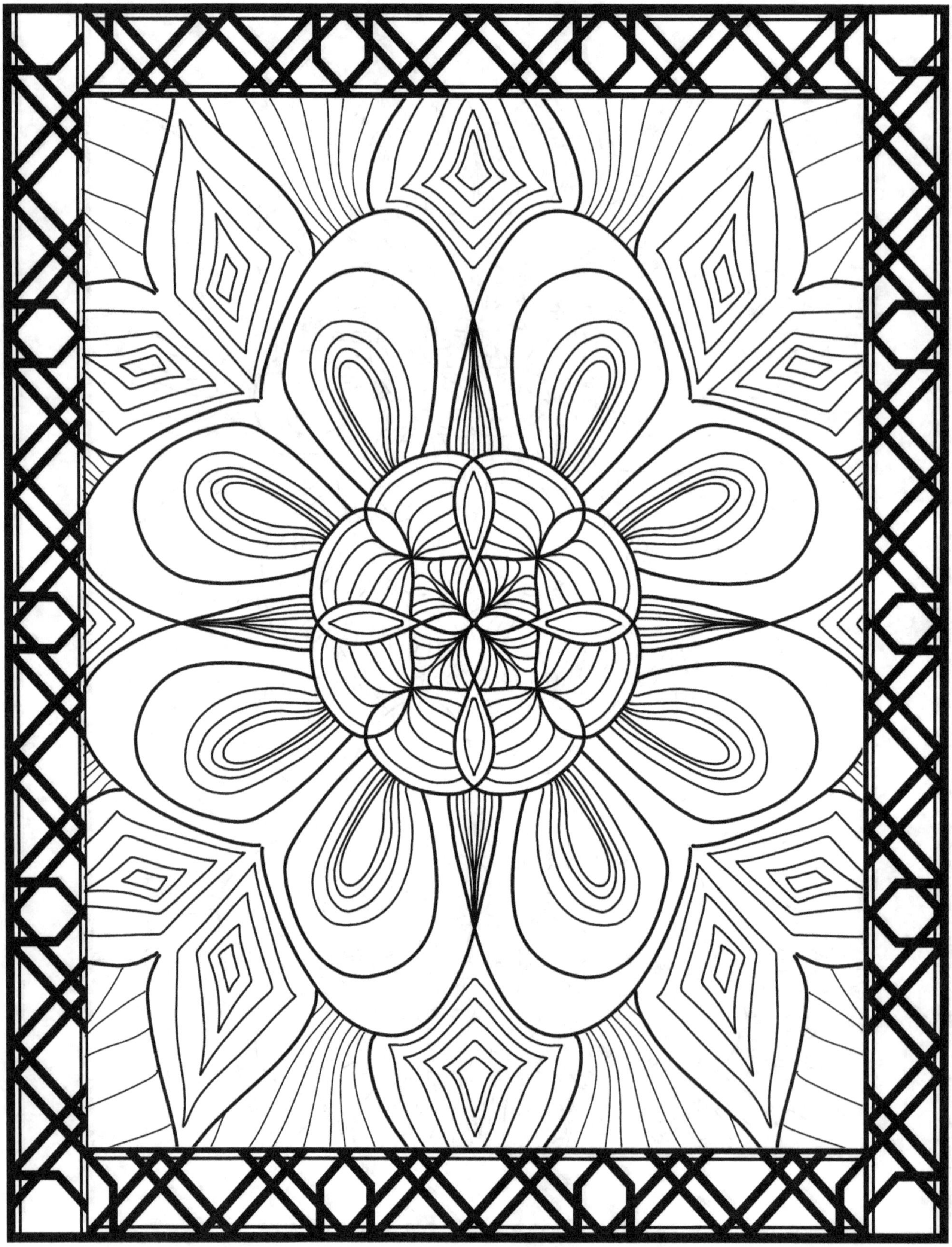

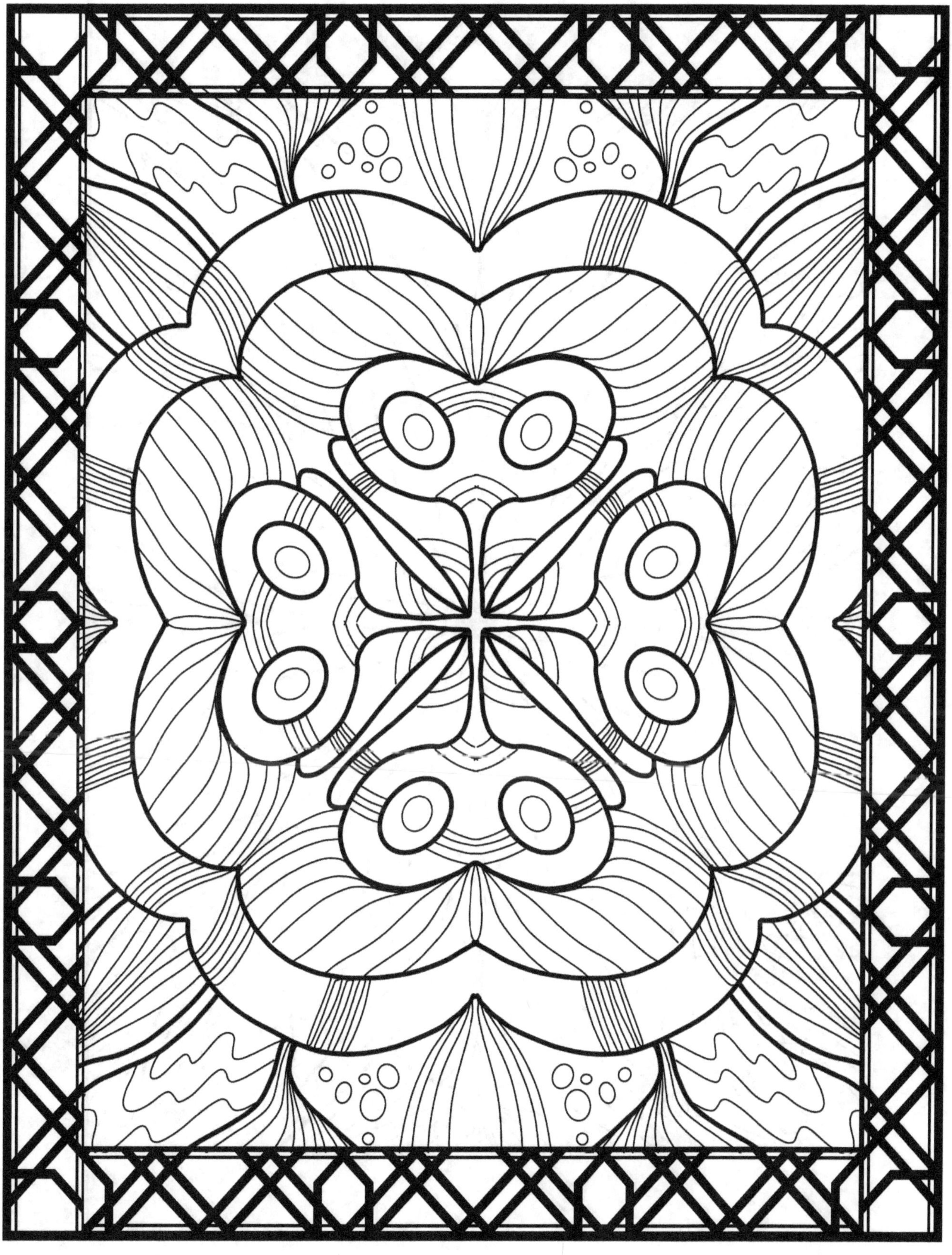

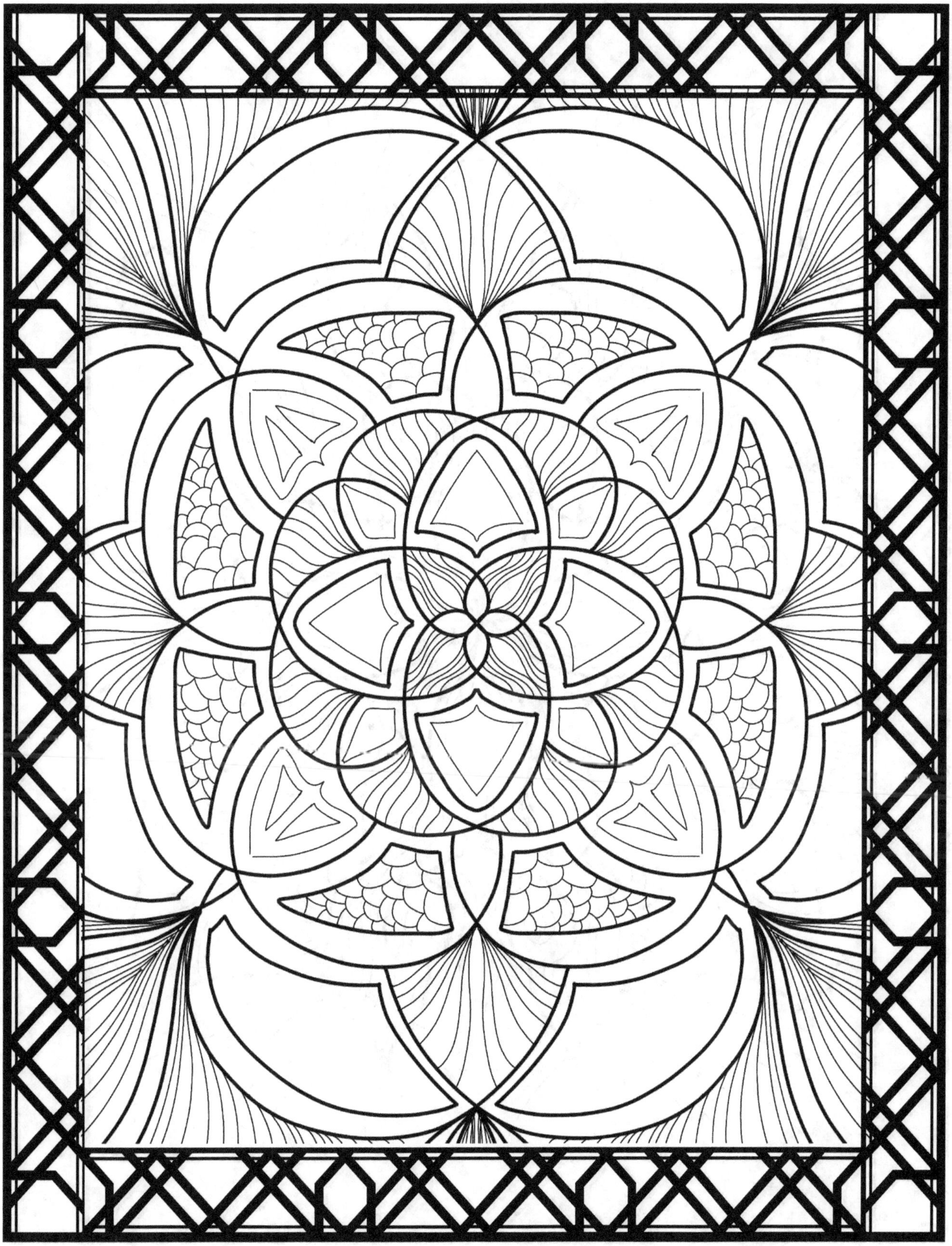

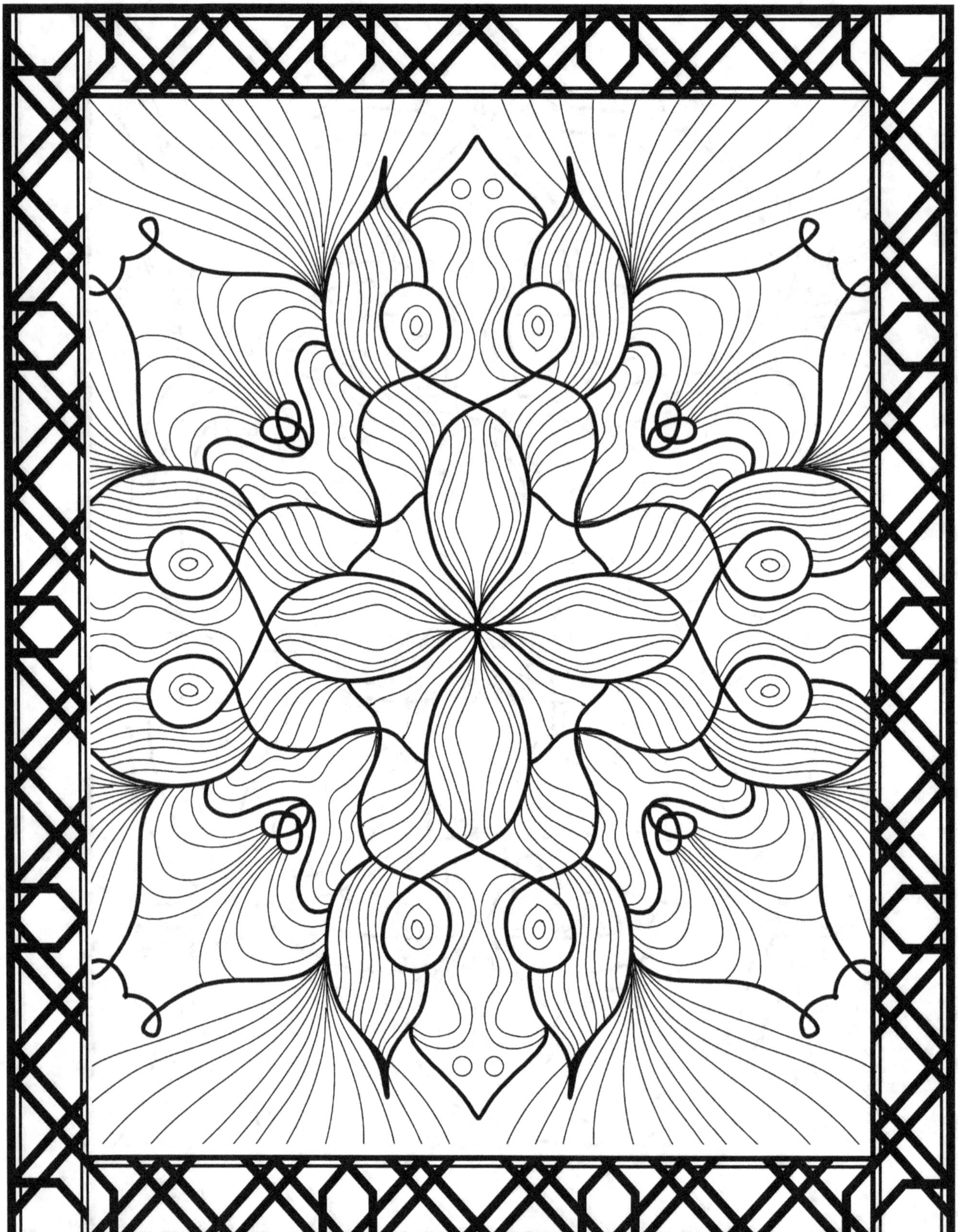

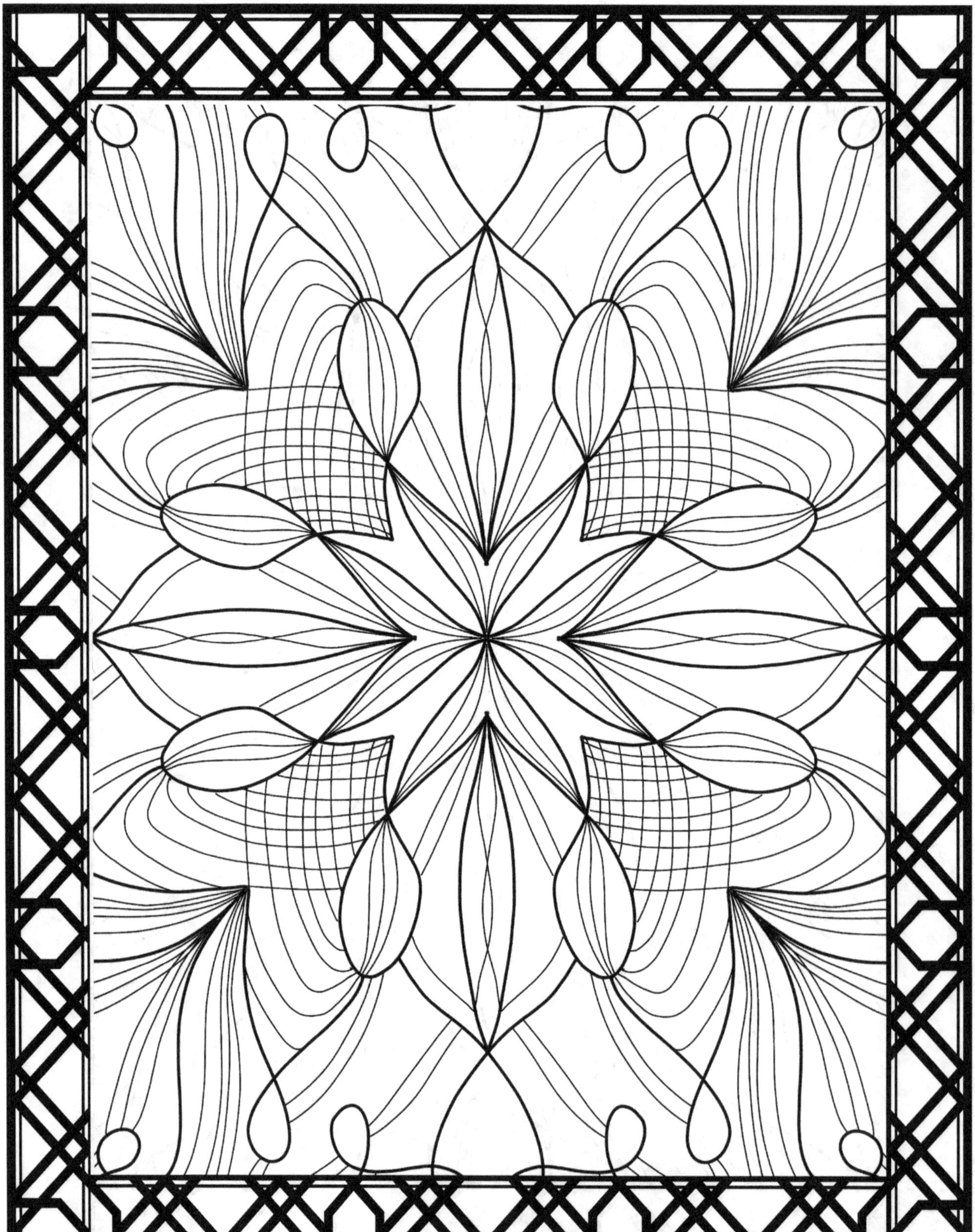

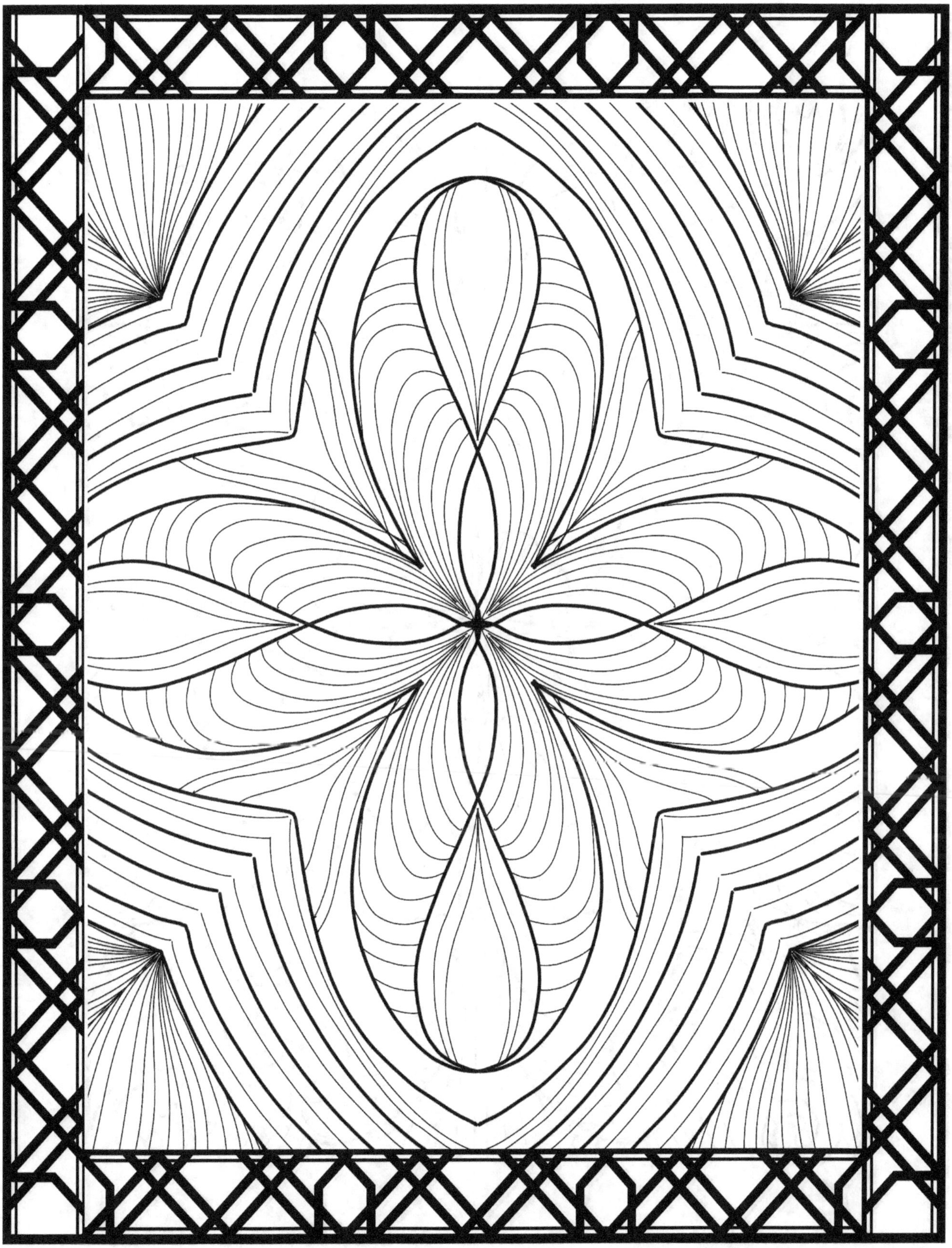

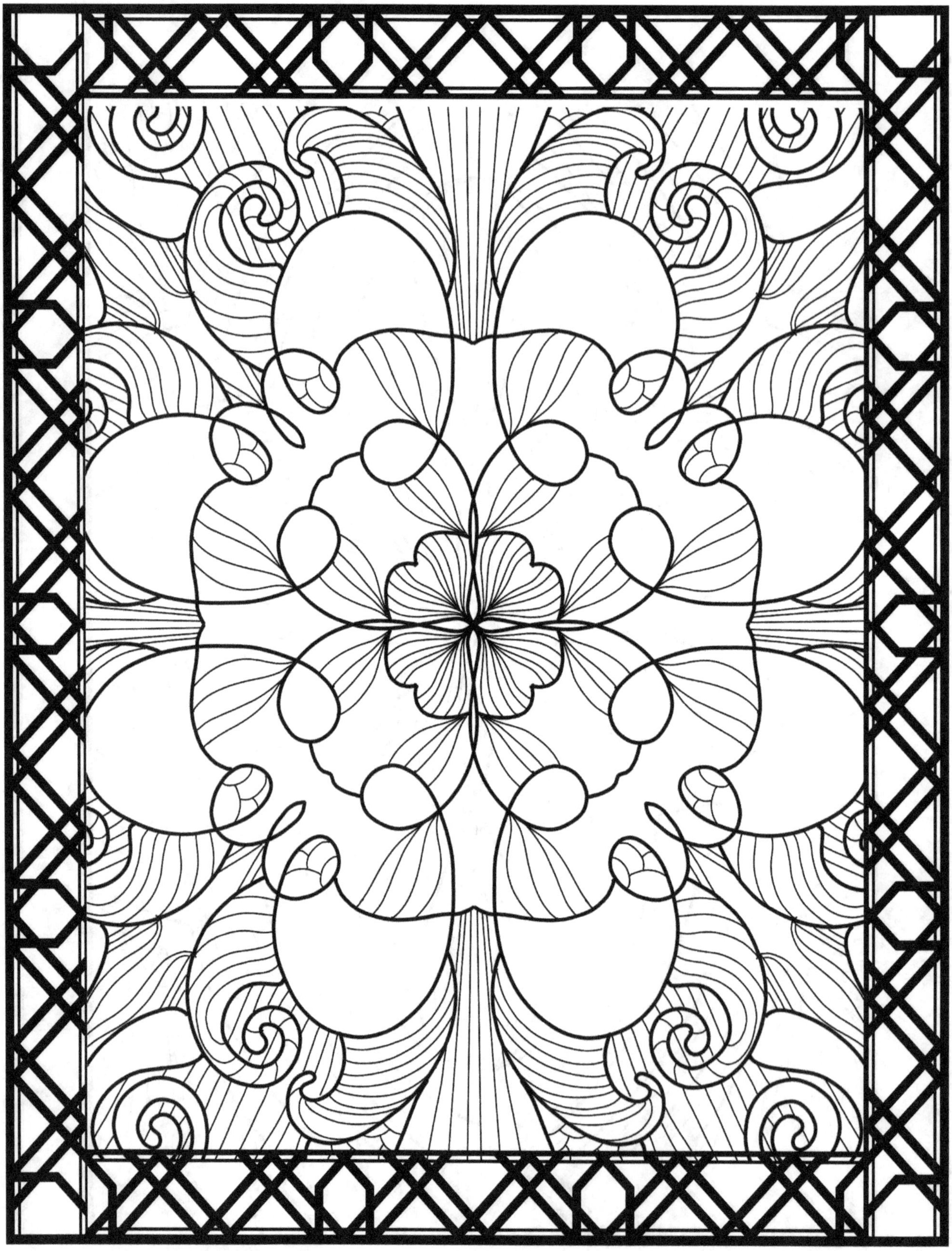

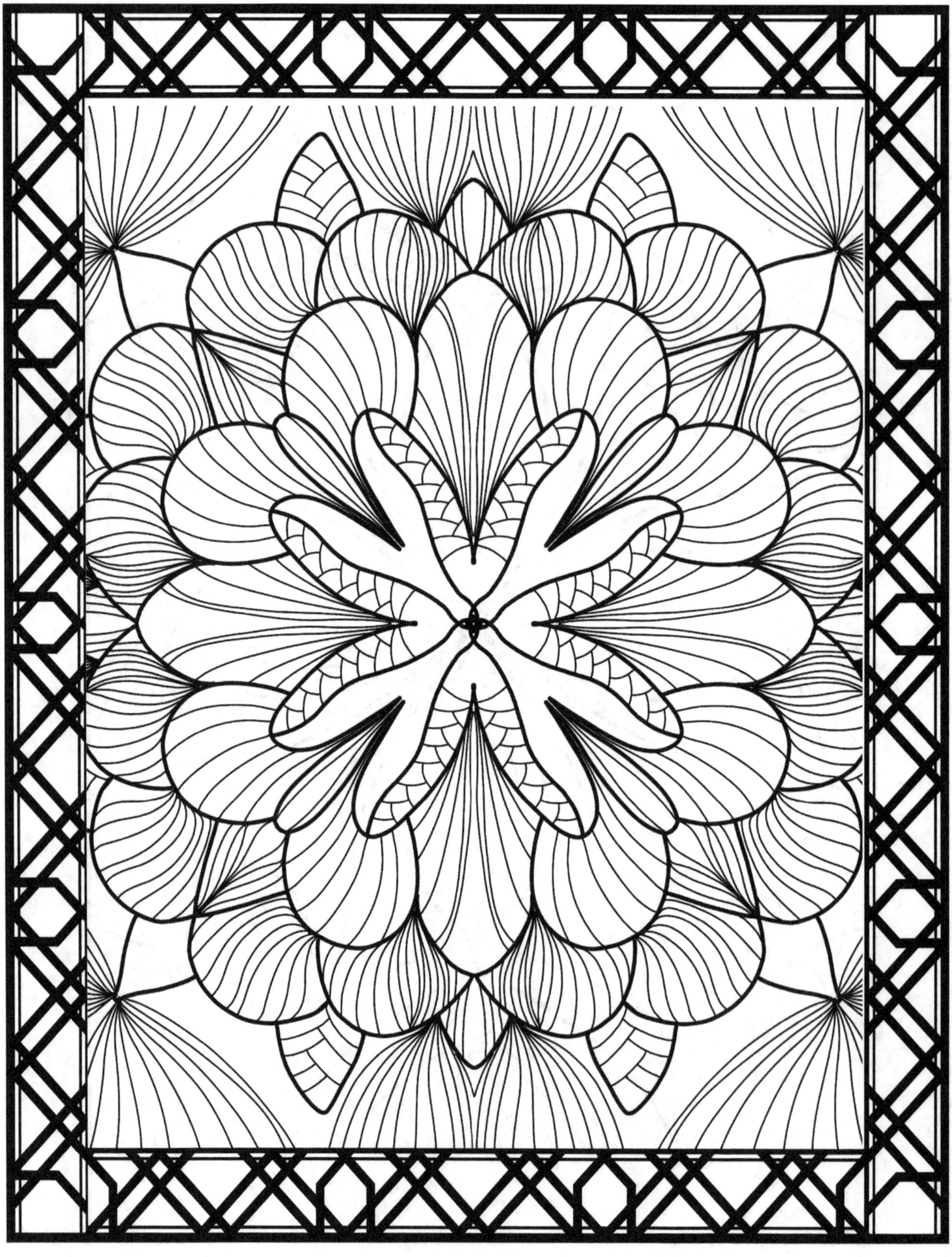

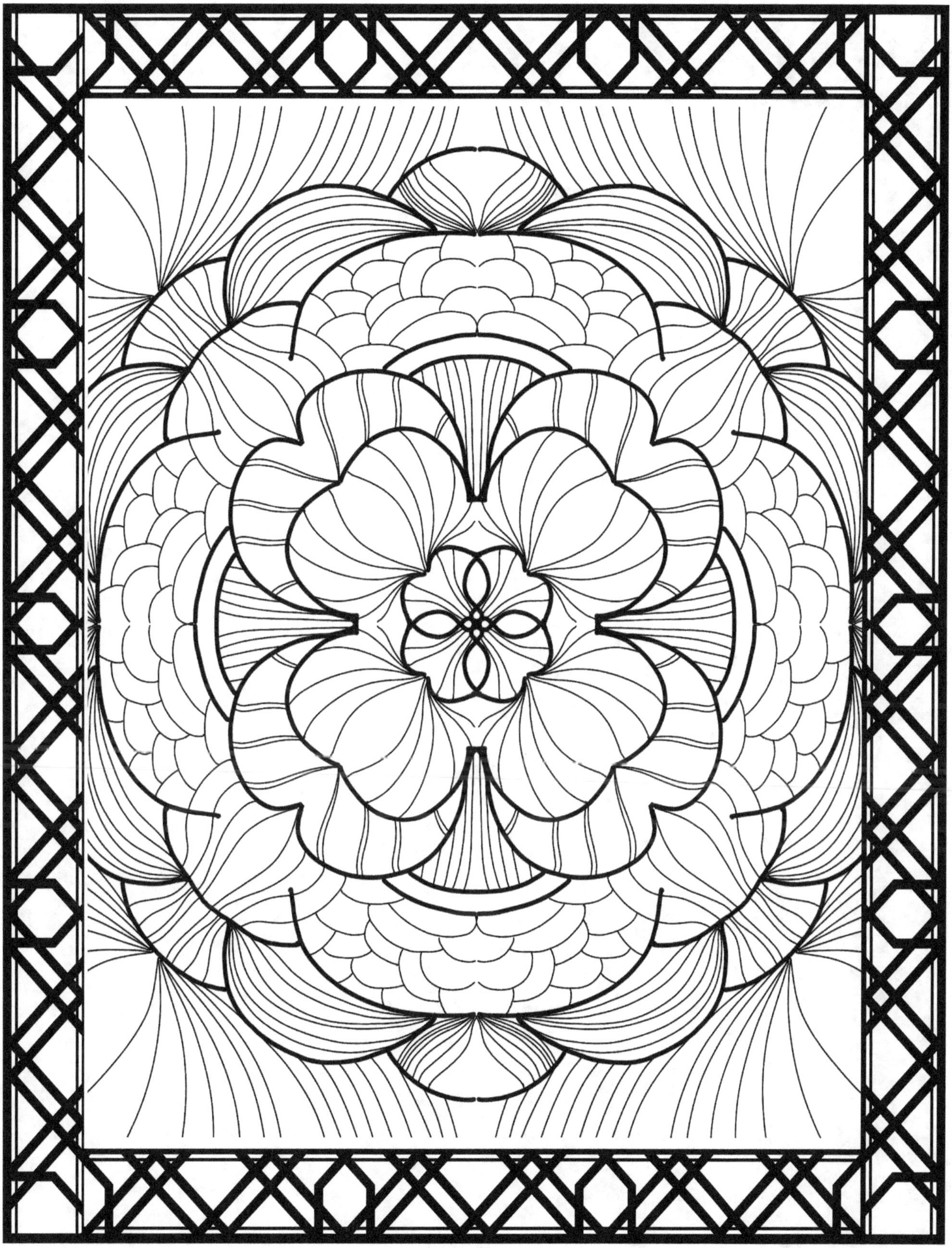

www.ingramcontent.com/pod-product-compliance
Lightning Source LLC
Chambersburg PA
CBHW080900170526
45158CB00009B/2782
* 9 7 8 1 0 7 3 1 3 9 3 8 5 *